D1717240

12 WOMEN IN
POLITICS

by Marne Ventura

STORY LIBRARY
MORE TO EXPLORE

www.12StoryLibrary.com

12-Story Library is an imprint of Bookstaves.

Photographs ©: Franmarie Metzler/PD, cover, 1; José Luiz Bernardes Ribeiro/CC4.0, 4; PHGCOM/PD, 4; PD, 5; Library of Congress, 6; Harris & Ewing/Library of Congress, 7; Levan Ramishvili/PD, 8; White House Photographic Office/PD, 9; Michael Germana/Everett Collection/Alamy, 10; Marcy Nighswander/Associated Press, 11; PD, 11; Gage Skidmore/ CC3.0, 12; Joseph Sohm/Shutterstock.com, 13; 360b/Shutterstock.com, 14; Pete Souza/ PD, 15; glen photo/Shutterstock.com, 16; 總統府/CC2.0, 17; United States Senate/PD, 18; Lorie Shaull/CC2.0, 19; Sergei Chuzavkov/Shutterstock.com, 20; Ivan Bandura/CC2.0, 21; Franmarie Metzler/PD, 22; Kalita Conley for Moms Clean Air Force/CC2.0, 23; Horacio Villalobos/Corbis/Getty Images, 24; Aliou Mbaye/Panapress/Newscom, 25; Governor-General of New Zealand/CC4.0, 26; James Dann/CC4.0, 27; Christchurch City Council Newsline/Kirk Hargreaves/CC4.0, 27; Yu Xunling/PD, 28; US Senate Historical Office/PD, 29

ISBN
9781632357816 (hardcover)
9781632358905 (paperback)
9781645820611 (ebook)

Library of Congress Control Number: 2019938618

Printed in the United States of America
September 2019

About the Cover
Deb Haaland in 2018.

Access free, up-to-date content on this topic plus a full digital version of this book. Scan the QR code on page 31 or use your school's login at 12StoryLibrary.com.

Table of Contents

Cleopatra VII: Ruler of Egypt

There are very few images of Cleopatra VII. This marble sculpture is from 46–44 BCE.

Cleopatra was the first ruler of Egypt to embrace its language and customs. Those before spoke Greek and followed Greek customs. They thought Egyptians were inferior. Cleopatra spoke nine languages. She understood politics and trade. Instead of using advisers, she worked directly with foreign rulers. She cared about Egypt and strived for peace and prosperity for her people.

In 48 BCE, Cleopatra's brother overthrew her. She fled to safety in Syria. At the same time, Julius Caesar took control of Rome. Rome needed grain from Egypt, so Caesar took over the palace there. Legend has it that Cleopatra snuck in, wrapped in a rug. To rule Egypt again, she needed

Cleopatra ruled Egypt for nearly 12 years. Born in 69 BCE, she was the last Greek ruler of a 300-year dynasty. Cleopatra was smart, charming, independent, and well educated. Her father died when she was 18. She and her younger brother became co-rulers.

A silver tetradrachm portraying Cleopatra VII.

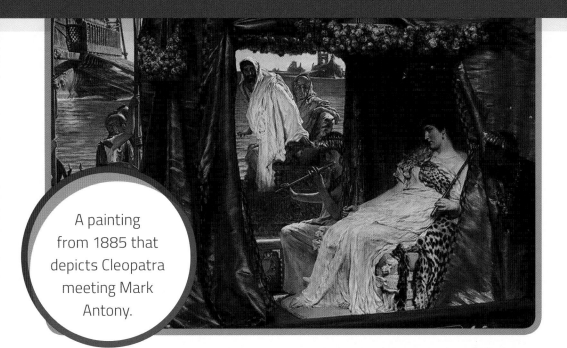

A painting from 1885 that depicts Cleopatra meeting Mark Antony.

the support of Rome. She and Caesar became friends. Cleopatra was restored to the throne.

Caesar returned to Rome. He was murdered in 44 BCE. Mark Antony and Octavian fought for control of Rome. Cleopatra went to Rome to meet with Mark Antony. She hoped to prevent Octavian from taking over Egypt. Antony and Cleopatra fell in love and became allies. In 30 BCE, the two lost a battle against Octavian. Both committed suicide rather than surrender.

3
Number of children Mark Antony and Cleopatra had together

- Cleopatra is wrongly portrayed in plays and films as a beautiful, wicked woman.
- Her strength was not beauty, but intelligence, education, and charisma.
- Her mother's identity is unknown, but historians say she may have been African.

THINK ABOUT IT

What were Cleopatra's strengths and weaknesses? Give a few examples.

Eleanor Roosevelt: American First Lady

Eleanor Roosevelt in 1933.

became interested in social work. At 18, she returned to New York and did volunteer work to help immigrant families. In 1905, she married her distant cousin Franklin Delano Roosevelt (FDR).

The Roosevelts had one daughter and five sons. In 1933, FDR became the 32nd president of the United States. He remained in office until his death in 1945. As First Lady, Eleanor worked tirelessly for social reform. During the Great Depression (1929–1939) and World War II (1939–1945), she traveled around the country and met with Americans. She looked for solutions to their problems and worked to make them happen. She asked people to write and ask her questions or tell her about problems. She wrote articles in newspapers and magazines to answer them. She donated her payment to charities.

Eleanor Roosevelt was a human rights activist. Born to a wealthy family in New York City in 1884, she was eight years old when her father died. Her mother and younger brother died before she was 10. Her grandmother became her guardian. She sent 15-year-old Eleanor to a school in England. Eleanor loved learning and traveling. She

Eleanor fought hard for human rights. She held weekly press conferences in the White House. She only allowed women reporters. This forced newspapers to hire women at a time when men were favored. She influenced FDR to appoint more women to his cabinet. In 1939, the Daughters of the American Revolution refused to let African American singer Marion Anderson perform in their auditorium. Roosevelt publicly resigned from the group.

3,000
Articles Eleanor Roosevelt wrote as First Lady

- After 12 years as First Lady, Eleanor worked for world peace through the United Nations.
- She chaired US President John F. Kennedy's Commission on the Status of Women.
- She worked on the Equal Pay Act in 1963.

Roosevelt (center) at one of her all-woman press conferences.

Margaret Thatcher: "Iron Lady"

Margaret Thatcher in 1988.

for education. She belonged to the Conservative Party. In 1979, she became the first female prime minister of the United Kingdom.

Thatcher's goal was to reduce the role of government. She believed people should take charge of their own well-being. For example, she ended a program that gave free milk to schoolchildren. She limited the power of trade unions that fought for more pay and better work conditions. She cut taxes.

Thatcher faced a range of problems as leader. Many British were not able to find jobs during her first term. Striking miners refused to work for nearly a year. Argentina tried to take away the Falkland Islands, a British territory. People called Thatcher the "Iron Lady" because she would not give in to her foes. Some admired her strength. Others found her strict and stiff. In 1984,

Margaret Thatcher was a lawyer and a politician. She was born in 1925 in Grantham, England. Her father was mayor of the town. Thatcher studied chemistry at Oxford University. She went on to study law. She became a member of Parliament, then secretary

terrorists tried to kill her by bombing a political meeting in Brighton. She was not hurt, but 5 people died and 34 were injured.

Thatcher was prime minister for nearly 12 years. Some say she put Britain's economy back on track. Others say she destroyed jobs for millions of workers.

3

Number of terms in a row Margaret Thatcher was elected prime minister

- For two decades, Thatcher was the only woman to lead a major Western democracy.
- She served from 1979–1990.
- She was a close ally of US President Ronald Reagan.

Thatcher meets with US President Ronald Reagan and his all-male cabinet in 1981.

Wilma Mankiller: Cherokee Chief

Wilma Mankiller was a Native American social worker. She was born in 1945 on tribal lands in Oklahoma. Her family of 13 had no electricity or plumbing. When she was 11, her family moved to San Francisco. Her father hoped to find work there and make a better life.

During the 1960s, Mankiller became involved in the Native American Rights movement. She went back to Oklahoma. She started a project where Cherokee people worked together to build a much-needed waterline. In 1983, she became deputy chief of the tribe. When the principal chief left for another job, she stepped up. She continued to serve after she won the next election. She was the first woman elected to serve as principal chief of the Cherokee Nation.

During her term, the number of Cherokee in the tribe tripled. Twice as many people had jobs. Mankiller oversaw the building of new housing and health centers. More infants survived. More children did well in school. In 1990, she signed a deal with the federal government. It gave control of millions of dollars to the Cherokee tribe. Other tribes use Mankiller's work as a model to improve life for their communities.

Wilma Mankiller in 2005.

Mankiller confers with Choctaw Chief Phillip Martin at an Indian affairs hearing with the Senate in 1989.

1998

Year when President Bill Clinton awarded Wilma Mankiller the Presidential Medal of Freedom

- Mankiller was inducted into the National Women's Hall of Fame in 1993.
- Her autobiography, *Mankiller: A Chief and Her People*, was published in 1993.
- She founded the Institute for Cherokee Literacy to keep Cherokee traditions alive.

THE WILMA MANKILLER FOUNDATION

Mankiller died in 2010. Today a group carries on her work. Their goal is to ensure Cherokee communities have fresh food and clean water. They help Cherokee people create neighborhood gardens. They teach them about canning and nutrition. They help communities set up waterline projects.

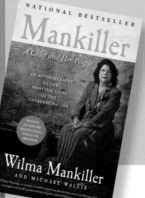

Hillary Rodham Clinton: American Politician

Hillary
Rodham Clinton
in 2016.

she was active in social work and student government. She earned a law degree from Yale in 1972.

Hillary and Bill Clinton married in 1975. She became First Lady of Arkansas when Bill became governor in 1978. She practiced law. She worked on programs to help children and the poor. She worked to improve education in Arkansas. Bill was elected US president in 1992. As First Lady, Clinton worked for better health care. She spoke out for human rights. In 2000, Clinton became the US senator from New York. In 2008, she became President Barack Obama's secretary of state.

Hillary Rodham Clinton is a lawyer, writer, speaker, and politician. She was born in 1947 in Chicago. Her father taught her the value of work. Her mother taught her to believe in herself and help others. From a young age,

In June of 2016, Clinton made history. She became the nominee for US president. She "broke the glass ceiling" as the first female nominee of a major party. Although she lost to Donald Trump, she paved the way for other women in politics.

65,853,516

Popular votes for Hillary Clinton in 2016 presidential election, nearly 3 million more than for Donald Trump

- Donald Trump got 304 electoral votes while Clinton got 227.
- Clinton has written three memoirs, *Hard Choices*, *Living History*, and *What Happened*.
- Her role model is Eleanor Roosevelt.

During her long career, Clinton has faced criticism as well as praise. Some people focused on her looks instead of her work. Some said a first lady shouldn't work in politics. As secretary of state, she was blamed for Americans killed in Libya. The FBI investigated her use of a personal email server to send government messages.

Clinton and US First Lady Michelle Obama at a campaign event in 2016.

STRONGER TOGETHER

hillaryclinton.com

Angela Merkel: Chancellor of Germany

For several years in the 2000s, Angela Merkel was the most powerful woman in the world. She was born in 1954. She grew up in communist East Germany. Merkel did well in school. She earned a PhD in chemistry. Some say she is a good leader because she thinks like a scientist. She studies facts to find the best choice.

In 1989, the Berlin Wall fell. Communist rule of East Germany ended. Merkel went to work for the Christian Democratic Union (CDU). This party's focus is social welfare and a free economy. It works to build friendships between countries in Europe and with the United States.

Since that time, Merkel has devoted her career to politics. She won a seat in Germany's parliament in 1990. She was minister for women and youth in 1991. By 1994, she was minister of the environment. In 2000, she became the first woman to lead the CDU. In 2005, Merkel became chancellor of Germany. She was the first woman, the first East German, and the youngest person to date to hold the office. In 2019, during her fourth term, she announced that she would step down in 2021. Merkel paved the way for future women in politics.

Angela Merkel in 2017.

Merkel with US President Barack Obama at a celebration of the fall of the Berlin Wall at the Brandenburg Gate in Berlin in 2013.

51

Angela Merkel's age when she became German chancellor

- Merkel helped improve a poor economy in Europe.
- She welcomes refugees from war zones.
- Helmut Kohl, who was chancellor before her, sometimes called her "the girl."

THE BERLIN WALL

Between 1949 and 1961, some 2.5 million people left East Germany to escape communism. Leaders built a wall in 1961. It was topped with barbed wire and guarded by armed soldiers. Those who tried to escape risked death. In October of 1989, a democracy movement forced the communists to take down the wall and open the country.

Tsai Ing-wen: First Female President of Taiwan

Tsai Ing-wen is a lawyer, scholar, and politician. She was born in 1956 to a wealthy family. She earned a law degree in 1978 in Taiwan. She went on to Cornell University in New York. Next, she earned a PhD in law in

1949
Year when Taiwan began ruling itself

- China's leaders still see Taiwan as their territory.
- Tsai works to advance the rights of women.
- She also endeavors to keep peace with China.

London. Until 2000, she was a law professor in Taiwan.

The president of Taiwan chose Tsai to be a trade adviser in the early 1990s. She left teaching for politics. She helped Taiwan join the World Trade Organization (WTO). In 2004, she joined the Democratic Progressive Party (DPP). She was elected to Taiwan's legislature. In 2006, she became vice premier of Taiwan. Then she became the first woman president of the DPP in 2008. In

Tsai Ing-wen in 2019.

Tsai attends her inaugural ceremony events in 2016.

2016, she became the first woman president of Taiwan.

China and Taiwan have been at odds for many years. China claims Taiwan is under their rule. Tsai wants Taiwan to be self-ruling. She strives for more trade between Taiwan and the world. This will prevent Taiwan from depending on China. It will also increase Taiwan's allies. Tsai works to unify her people, who have been torn apart by fighting in the past.

TAIWAN AND CHINA

Since 1624, Taiwan has been controlled by the Dutch, then the Chinese, then the Japanese. After World War II (1939–1945), China took over until 1949. Since then, leaders of China and Taiwan have disagreed about the government of Taiwan. China says that Taiwan is part of their country. Taiwan's leaders are working to make Taiwan an independent country.

Amy Klobuchar: US Senator

2006, Klobuchar served as a county attorney in Minnesota.

In 2006, Klobuchar became the first woman elected as a US senator from Minnesota. She was reelected in 2012 and 2018. As senator, she got funding to rebuild an important bridge in Minnesota. She got funding for farmers and veterans in need.

7

Number of Klobuchar's bills that became law during the 115th Congress

- Klobuchar ranked No. 1 for most bills (92) introduced during the 115th Congress.
- She supports former President Barack Obama's idea to make community college free.
- Many Republicans in Minnesota support Klobuchar, a Democrat.

Amy Klobuchar is a lawyer and politician. She was born in 1960 in Minnesota. Her father was a journalist and her mother was a teacher. Klobuchar finished high school and college at the top of her class. She earned a law degree from the University of Chicago. She worked for Walter Mondale when he was vice president under Jimmy Carter. From 1998 to

She helped rewrite the Senate's ethics rules. She got more funds for science, technology, engineering, and math training in schools.

In February of 2019, Klobuchar joined the race for the 2020 Democratic presidential nomination. Her plan is to update America's infrastructure. She wants to improve mental health services. She supports more laws to deal with climate change.

INFRASTRUCTURE

Infrastructure is the buildings, people, and systems that keep a community working. Roads enable people to get to school and work. Tunnels and bridges let them go under or over roads or waterways. Sewers carry waste away. Phone lines allow people to communicate. Electricity keeps lights and appliances working. These are all examples of infrastructure.

Klobuchar makes her announcement to run for president in 2020.

Yulia Tymoshenko: Ukrainian Prime Minister

Yulia Tymoshenko is a businesswoman and politician. She was born in 1960. She earned a degree in economics in 1984. In 1995, she became wealthy as president of a gas company. In 1996, she was elected to the Ukrainian parliament. She became deputy prime minister for fuel and

3
Number of times Yulia Tymoshenko ran for president of Ukraine and lost

- Tymoshenko was the first woman to be prime minister of Ukraine. She served from 2005 and again from 2007–2010.
- She was nicknamed the "gas princess" after owning a successful energy company.
- She ran for president in 2010, 2014, and 2019.

Yulia Tymoshenko in 2019.

energy in 1999. Two years later, she was arrested and jailed for corruption. Tymoshenko claims her enemies made up false charges against her. Some say she was being punished for being pro-democracy. The charges were later dropped.

Tymoshenko's supporters march for her to be freed in 2013.

In 2004, Ukraine was on the brink of civil war. Tymoshenko became a leader in the Orange Revolution. Her group accused the current president of corruption. They worked to elect a new president. This candidate was poisoned. He lived, but his face was scarred. The two candidates tied. After two weeks of protest, Tymoshenko's candidate took office. He named Tymoshenko prime minister in 2005. After nine months, she was accused of corruption and fired.

Tymoshenko's party won the election in 2006. She was made prime minister again in 2007. She worked for democracy. In 2011, she was again accused of corruption. She was sentenced to seven years in jail. Europe, the United States, and Russia questioned whether her charges were fair. In 2014, a decision by the European Court of Human Rights led to her release.

THINK ABOUT IT

Many politicians face criticism and unfair treatment by their opponents. Would you want to be a politician? Why or why not?

Deb Haaland:
Pueblo Congresswoman

Deb Haaland is an attorney and politician. Her father was a Marine hero. Her mother is a Navy veteran. Haaland is a member of the Pueblo of Laguna. She is a 35th generation New Mexican.

Haaland became a single mother at a young age. She worked at her daughter's pre-school. She relied on food stamps and took out student loans to earn a law degree. She ran a small business making and selling salsa. Later she oversaw a tribal gaming company in New Mexico. She was also a tribal leader who helped provide services for adults with disabilities.

In 2014, Haaland became the first Native American woman elected to lead a state political party. She worked for President Barack Obama's campaign. She helped fight for clean water at the Standing Rock reservation in North Dakota. In 2018, Haaland became one of the first two Native American women elected to Congress.

Haaland wants to create more and better-paying clean energy jobs in New Mexico. She wants to make it easier for New Mexicans to start

Deb Haaland in 2018.

small businesses. She wants to improve education and end poverty. For the first time, young Native American women have a role model in Congress.

Haaland speaks at a Moms Clean Air Force gathering in 2019 about the need for urgent action to reduce air pollution.

22
Number of Native Americans elected to the US Congress since 1789

- That's 22 out of more than 12,300 people elected since the first US Congress met.
- Native Americans weren't US citizens until 1924.
- They couldn't vote in New Mexico until 1962.

THE 2018 ELECTIONS

The 2018 midterm elections were historic for women. Ninety-six female candidates won in the House of Representatives. Thirty-one were newly elected. Michigan Democrat Rashida Tlaib and Minnesota Democrat Ilhan Omar became the first Muslim women elected to the House.

Aminata Touré: Prime Minister of Senegal

Aminata Touré is a human rights activist and politician. Born in Senegal in 1962, she was the daughter of a doctor and a midwife. She went to public school in Senegal. She played soccer in Dakar. She earned a PhD in business in France.

After college, Touré worked for human rights and women's rights in Senegal. She worked for the United Nations in New York in the human rights department. She fought for

3
Number of languages Aminata Touré speaks

- Touré is fluent in English, French, and Wolof.
- She has been an important role model for women in politics in Senegal.
- She speaks out for better living conditions in rural Senegal.

Aminata Touré in 2019.

Touré addresses the Senegal National Assembly in 2013.

women's health care. In 2012, she became Senegal's justice minister. She was known and admired for fighting against government corruption.

In 2013, Touré was appointed prime minister of Senegal. She was the second female to serve in the job. Women's groups celebrated the event. They also criticized Touré for appointing only four women to her 32-member cabinet. In 2014, Touré lost an election in Dakar. This ended her term as prime minister. She now serves as a special envoy of Macky Sall, president of Senegal. She speaks for groups that support human rights and women's health.

LIFE IN SENEGAL

Compared with much of Africa, Senegal has a stable government. The standard of living gets better each year. Most people make a living by farming. Although much of the work is still done by hand, the government is working to help farmers get machinery. Over half of the country has electricity. Over 92 percent of children up to the age of 16 are enrolled in public school.

Jacinda Ardern: World's Youngest Female Head of Government

Jacinda Ardern in 2019.

a college degree in 2001. In 1999, she joined the Labour Party. After college, she worked for Helen Clark, New Zealand's second female prime minister.

In 2005, Ardern went to London. She spent two years working for British Prime Minister Tony Blair. She helped businesses and government work together. In 2007, she became president of the International Union of Socialist Youth. She traveled throughout Africa and the East. In 2008, she was elected to New Zealand's House of Representatives. She was 28 and the youngest member.

Jacinda Ardern is a New Zealand politician. She was born in 1980 in a small town. Her father was a police officer. She was inspired to enter politics by seeing Maori people who were living in poverty. The Maori are the indigenous people of New Zealand. Ardern wanted to help. She earned

THINK ABOUT IT

Needy Maori in Jacinda Ardern's community inspired her to go into politics. Who would you want to help if you were a politician?

Ardern worked to make learning Maori mandatory in public schools. She worked for laws that address climate change.

In 2017, Ardern was elected prime minister of New Zealand. She called for free college and more programs to help children in need. In March 2019, a terrorist attack on two New Zealand mosques left 50 dead and 50 injured. The shooter was a racist who was protesting immigration. Ardern was widely praised for her grace in comforting the victims. She wore a hijab to meet with the survivors. She also banned most semiautomatic weapons in New Zealand.

11
Number of countries led by women in 2018, out of almost 200

- Jacinda Ardern gave birth to a daughter in 2018.
- She uses social media to reach out to her people.
- She supported Facebook's removal of videos of the mosque attacks.

Ardern visited the Muslim community immediately following the terrorist attack.

Out of the Shadows

Hatshepsut

Born in 1508 BCE, Hatshepsut was the daughter of Egyptian Pharoah Thutmose I and his queen, Ahmose. When her father died, she and her younger brother were the heirs to the throne. At that time, women oversaw young male rulers until the males were old enough to rule alone. Instead, Hatshepsut declared herself pharaoh and ruled for 20 years.

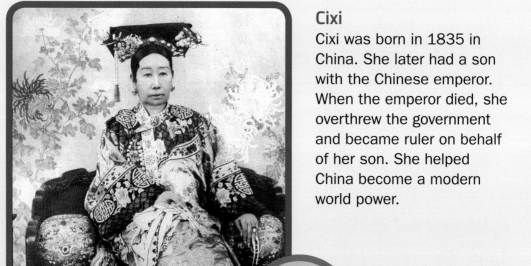

Cixi

Cixi was born in 1835 in China. She later had a son with the Chinese emperor. When the emperor died, she overthrew the government and became ruler on behalf of her son. She helped China become a modern world power.

Cixi circa 1890.

Nzinga Mbande

Nzinga Mbande was queen of the Mbundu people in Central Africa. She was born around 1583 in modern-day Angola, where her father was king of the Ndongo people. After his death, the Portuguese took control of the kingdom. Mbande fought to regain power and stop the slave trade.

Margaret Chase Smith

Born in 1897 in Maine, Margaret Chase Smith became a role model for women in politics. She was the first woman to win a seat in the US House and the US Senate. She served in Congress from 1939 to 1973.

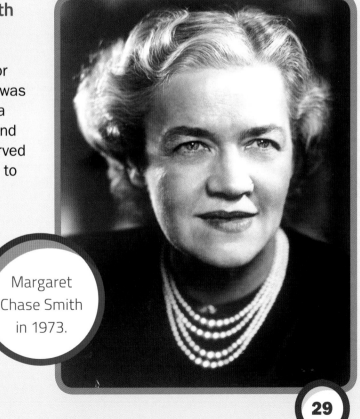

Margaret Chase Smith in 1973.

Glossary

activist
A person who takes action for political change.

chancellor
In Germany and Austria, the top government official.

communism
A system where the government, rather than individual people, own and control things.

corruption
Dishonest or illegal behavior.

dynasty
Rulers from the same family.

endeavor
To work hard at something; to strive.

envoy
A representative or messenger.

fluent
Able to speak a language very well.

hijab
A head cover worn by some Muslim women.

immigrant
A person who comes to a country to live there.

indigenous
Living naturally in a particular place or region; native to that place or region.

mosque
A place where Muslims worship.

parliament
In the United Kingdom, the branch of government where laws are made.

prosperity
Wealth, success, well-being.

welfare
The state of doing well, being healthy and successful.

Read More

Alexander, Heather. *Who Is Hillary Clinton?* Who Was? New York: Penguin Workshop, 2016.

Carr, Simonetta. *Cleopatra and Ancient Egypt for Kids: Her Life and World.* Chicago, IL: Chicago Review Press, 2018.

Gimple, Diane. *12 Immigrants Who Made American Politics Great.* A Nation of Immigrants. Mankato, MN: 12-Story Library, 2019.

Henzel, Cynthia Kennedy. *Jacinda Ardern: Prime Minister of New Zealand.* World Leaders. Lake Elmo, MN: Focus Readers, 2019.

Visit 12StoryLibrary.com

Scan the code or use your school's login at **12StoryLibrary.com** for recent updates about this topic and a full digital version of this book. Enjoy free access to:

- Digital ebook
- Breaking news updates
- Live content feeds
- Videos, interactive maps, and graphics
- Additional web resources

Note to educators: Visit 12StoryLibrary.com/register to sign up for free premium website access. Enjoy live content plus a full digital version of every 12-Story Library book you own for every student at your school.

Index

About the Author

Marne Ventura has written over 100 books for children. A former elementary school teacher, she holds a master's degree in education from the University of California. Marne and her husband live on the central coast of California.